The Six-Figure Copywriting Blueprint

Proven Strategies for Writing Compelling Copy, Landing Dream Clients, and Leaving the 9-to-5 Grind Behind

Benjamin Preston

Contents

1. Introduction   1

2. The Fundamentals of Writing Great Sales Copy   3

3. Adapting Classic Copywriting Techniques for Today   6

4. Crafting Irresistible Offers & Lead Magnets to Build Your List   9

5. Writing High-Converting Email Campaigns   13

6. Secrets of Writing Lucrative Video Sales Letters (VSLs)   18

7. Mastering the Art of the Long-Form Sales Page   23

8. How to Write Ads That Stop the Scroll on Social Media   29

9. Becoming a Master Storyteller to Engage Today's Distracted Audiences   36

10. Productivity Hacks to Write More Copy in Less Time   43

11. The Business of Freelance Copywriting: Getting Clients, Setting Rates, Delivering Results   50

12. Conclusion: Your Roadmap to Copywriting Success & Leaving the 9-to-5 Behind   56

Chapter One

Introduction

L et's cut to the chase - you're here because you're tired of the daily grind, right? Waking up to the sound of your alarm blaring, dragging yourself out of bed, and spending the next 8 hours (or more) trapped in a cubicle, making someone else's dreams a reality. Sound familiar?

Well, what if I told you there's a way to escape that soul-crushing routine and build a life of freedom, flexibility, and financial independence? And no, this isn't some pyramid scheme or MLM nonsense - I'm talking about a legit, in-demand skill that can earn you some serious cash.

That skill? Copywriting.

Now, before you start thinking, "Writing isn't really for me," hear me out. Copywriting isn't about crafting the next Great American Novel or penning flowery poems. It's about understanding what makes people tick, tapping into their deepest desires and fears, and using the power of words to persuade and inspire action.

In other words, it's the ultimate superpower for anyone looking to succeed in today's digital world.

And the best part? You don't need a fancy degree, years of experience, or even a natural "gift" for writing to become a skilled copywriter. All you need is a willingness to learn, a drive to succeed, and maybe a slightly unhealthy caffeine habit (trust me, it helps).

Throughout this book, I'll be sharing the exact strategies, techniques, and mindset shifts that have allowed countless people just like you to build thriving freelance copywriting businesses and leave the 9-to-5 grind behind. We'll dive into the core of writing persuasive copy, explore the most lucrative niches and formats, and uncover the secrets to landing high-paying clients and scaling your income.

But fair warning: this isn't a fluffy, feel-good read filled with empty promises and generic advice. I'm going to give it to you straight - building a successful freelance business takes hard work, dedication, and a willingness to keep pushing forward even when things get tough.

But if you're ready to put in the effort and take control of your life, then buckle up. By the time you finish this book, you'll have all the tools, knowledge, and confidence you need to start your journey as an in-demand, well-paid copywriter.

So, grab a coffee (or a Red Bull, if that's more your speed), find a comfy spot, and let's dive in.

The Fundamentals of Writing Great Sales Copy

Alright, let's get down to the heart of writing copy that converts. And no, I'm not talking about using sleazy, manipulative tactics or churning out generic, cookie-cutter content. I'm talking about mastering the art of understanding what makes your audience tick and crafting messages that resonate with their deepest desires and emotions.

First up, let's talk about what really drives human behavior. **Spoiler alert:** it's not logic or rationality. Nope, we're all driven by our emotions, whether we like to admit it or not. And as a copywriter, your job is to tap into those emotions and use them to your advantage.

How do you do that, you ask? It all starts with crafting irresistible headlines and hooks that grab your reader's attention and refuse to let go. Because, if your headline doesn't stop them in their tracks and make them think, "Ooh, I gotta read this," then the rest of your copy might as well be written in ancient Greek.

But a great headline is just the beginning. Once you've got their attention, you need to keep them engaged by highlighting the life-changing benefits of your offer. And no, I'm not talking about boring, generic benefits like "saves you time", "new light-weight design" or "easy to use." I'm talking about the kind of benefits that make your reader feel like they've just discovered the secret to happiness, success, and eternal youth.

Think about it: what's really going to motivate someone to whip out their credit card and buy what you're selling? Is it the fact that your product has 27 different features and a sleek design? Or is it the promise that it will help them lose 20 pounds, find their soulmate, or finally start that business they've been dreaming about?

You guessed it - it's the latter. So, when you're writing your copy, focus on painting a vivid picture of how your offer will transform your reader's life in a meaningful way. Make them feel the excitement, the joy, the relief that comes with solving their biggest problems and achieving their deepest desires.

But none of that matters if your reader doesn't trust you. In today's cynical, skeptical world, establishing trust and credibility is more important than ever. And the best way to do that? Through social proof and honest, transparent copy.

That means including testimonials, case studies, and other forms of third-party validation that show your reader that other people just like them have gotten awesome results from your offer. It also means being upfront about what your product can and can't do, and not making any ridiculous, over-the-top claims that sound too good to be true.

Finally, none of this matters if you don't inspire your reader to take action. And that means crafting clear, compelling calls-to-action that make it easy and risk-free for them to say "yes" to your offer.

Whether it's a "Buy Now" button, a "Sign Up Today" form, or a "Schedule Your Free Consultation" link, your call-to-action should be impossible to miss and even harder to resist. And don't be afraid to get creative with your CTAs - sometimes, a little humor or personality can go a long way in getting your reader to take that final step.

So there you have it - the fundamentals of writing great sales copy. Master these principles, and you'll be well on your way to crafting copy that not only grabs attention and engages your reader but also inspires them to take action and transform their lives in a meaningful way.

Chapter Three

Adapting Classic Copywriting Techniques for Today

Alright, so you've mastered the basics of crafting killer sales copy. But let's be real - the game has changed big time. Long-form sales letters and old-school direct mail campaigns aren't exactly lighting the world on fire these days. If you want to crush it in today's digital landscape, you need to know how to take those tried-and-true copywriting techniques and adapt them for the online world, where attention is the most precious commodity.

First, you've got to become a master at writing for the skimmers and scanners out there. Let's face it - most people aren't going to hang on your every word like you're the second coming of Shakespeare. They're going to skim, scan, and scroll until something jumps out and grabs them by the eyeballs.

So how do you make sure your message cuts through the noise? It all comes down to formatting, my friend. Short paragraphs, bullet points, subheadings - these are your secret weapons when it comes to writing for the web. Break your copy up into bite-sized chunks that are easy to digest, and use plenty of white space to give your reader's eyes a break from the wall of text.

But it's not just about making your copy look pretty - it's about making it engaging and persuasive across every platform out there. Whether you're crafting a landing page, firing off an email, or dropping a social media post, you need to know how to write copy that grabs attention, sparks an emotional connection, and makes people want to take action.

And one of the most powerful ways to do that is through storytelling, baby. Humans have been hardwired for stories since the dawn of time - we can't get enough of them. When you can weave a compelling narrative into your copy, you create an emotional bond with your reader that goes way beyond just spitting facts and figures at them.

Think about it - would you rather read some bland, generic product description, or a juicy, engaging story about how that product completely transformed someone's life? I know which one I'm picking every time.

But here's the thing - even the greatest story ever told won't mean anything if it's not optimized for how people actually consume content online these days. And right now, that means mobile devices and attention spans that make a goldfish look like a Mensa member.

So how do you make sure your message hits them right between the eyes, even when they're scrolling through their phone on the toilet? It's all about being concise, clear, and compelling as hell. Keep your sentences short and punchy. Get to the damn point already. And always, always, always keep your reader's needs and desires front and center.

Oh, and don't even think about sleeping on the power of visuals. A well-placed image or video can do wonders for breaking up your copy and keeping your reader glued to the screen. Just make sure it's relevant, high-quality, and actually adds something to your message instead of just being there for the sake of it.

So there you have it - the key to dragging those classic copywriting techniques kicking and screaming into the digital age. Master the art of writing for the skimmers and scanners, craft copy that engages and persuades no matter where it's showing up, harness the power of storytelling, and optimize the hell out of your message for mobile and microscopic attention spans.

Chapter Four

Crafting Irresistible Offers & Lead Magnets to Build Your List

If you want to build a list of rabid fans who can't wait to throw their money at you, you need to nail your offers and lead magnets. And I'm not talking about some weak-ass "free report" that rehashes the same tired info they've seen a million times. I'm talking about crafting irresistible, drool-worthy offers that make your target audience feel instant dopamine spikes.

But before you even think about slapping together a lead magnet, you need to get inside your audience's head. I mean really dig deep and figure out what keeps them up at night, what they're secretly fantasizing about, and what would make their lives a hell of a lot easier.

Because once you know their pain points and deepest desires better than they know themselves, you can create an offer that's tailored specifically to them.

For example, let's say you're targeting busy moms who are struggling to lose the baby weight. They don't need another generic "**10 Tips for Healthy Eating**" PDF. They need something that shows you understand their unique challenges, like a "**7-Day Meal Plan for Melting Away Stubborn Baby Weight, Even If You Have Zero Free Time.**" See the difference?

But crafting a mouthwatering offer is just the first step. You also need to position yourself as the go-to authority in your niche, the one person who can guide them to the promised land. How? By overdelivering on value in your lead magnet. We're talking actionable, step-by-step advice that they can implement right away for real results. None of that vague, wishy-washy nonsense that leaves them feeling more confused than when they started.

So let's say you're creating a lead magnet for aspiring freelance writers. Instead of some generic "**How to Make Money Writing Online**" guide, give them a "**Proven Pitching Template for Landing Your First $1K Writing Gig in 30 Days or Less.**" Include real examples, detailed breakdowns, and insider tips that showcase your expertise. By the time they're done consuming your lead magnet, they should be thinking, "Damn, this guy/gal really knows their stuff. I need more!"

But even the juiciest offer and most value-packed lead magnet won't do you any good if your opt-in page looks like a steaming pile of garbage. So how do you design a high-converting opt-in page that practically forces people to hand over their email address?

First, keep it simple and laser-focused. Your headline should clearly state the big benefit of your lead magnet, and your subheadline should reinforce it with a specific promise. For example: **"Discover the 5-Step Formula for Doubling Your Conversion Rates in 30 Days (Without Spending a Dime on Ads)."**

Next, make sure your opt-in form is impossible to miss. Use a contrasting color, keep the fields to a minimum (name and email is usually plenty), and use a clear, benefit-driven call-to-action button like **"Send Me the Formula!"** instead of something lame like **"Submit."**

Oh, and don't forget the power of social proof. Slap some glowing testimonials or impressive numbers (like **"Join 10,000+ Happy Subscribers!"**) right next to your opt-in form to give people that extra nudge.

Finally, once you've got your irresistible offer and high-converting opt-in page ready to go, you need to drive some damn traffic to it. And not just any traffic - laser-targeted, ready-to-buy traffic.

One of the best ways to do this is through social media ads. Facebook and Instagram allow you to get super granular with your targeting, so you can put your lead magnet in front of the exact right people. Just make sure your ad creative and copy are on point, with a clear value proposition and a strong call-to-action.

You can also tap into other people's audiences by partnering up for a joint venture or doing a list swap. Just make sure you're partnering with people who have a similar target audience and a solid reputation. The last thing you want is to blast your carefully crafted lead magnet to a bunch of freebie-seeking tire-kickers.

So there you have it - the key to crafting irresistible offers and lead magnets that'll have people tripping over themselves to join your list. Figure out what your audience really wants, overdeliver on value, design an opt-in page that converts like crazy, and drive the right traffic to it.

Do all that, and you'll be well on your way to building a loyal tribe of email subscribers who can't wait to buy whatever you're selling. And that, my friend, is how you print money.

Chapter Five

Writing High-Converting Email Campaigns

So you've got a list of hot leads just itching to throw their hard-earned cash at you. Congrats, you're halfway there! But now comes the really juicy part - writing the kind of email campaigns that'll make those leads whip out their wallets.

But before you start firing off emails, you need to take a step back and map out a strategy. And I'm not talking about some half-assed "send a newsletter once a month" kind of strategy. I'm talking about a full-blown, multi-step email marketing plan that'll take your subscribers on a wild ride from "who the hell are you?" to "shut up and take my money!"

Here's how you do it: First, you segment your list based on where they are in your sales funnel. Are they fresh-faced newbies who need a little nurturing? Or are they hot leads who are ready to buy? Once you know who you're talking to, you can craft the perfect email sequence to guide them to the promised land (aka your checkout page).

For the newbies, you might start with a welcome series that introduces them to your brand, shares your best content, and starts building that know-like-trust factor. Hit them with a mix of valuable info, entertaining stories, and subtle pitches for your entry-level offers.

For the warmer leads, it's time to turn up the heat with some harder-hitting promos. But don't just slam them with "BUY NOW!" emails - you've got to finesse it a bit. Weave in some social proof, scarcity tactics, and irresistible bonuses to sweeten the deal.

Now, let's talk about the emails themselves. If your subject lines are putting people to sleep, it doesn't matter how good the rest of your email is - it ain't getting opened. So how do you write subject lines that practically beg to be clicked?

First, keep 'em short and punchy. Aim for 7-10 words max, and put the most tantalizing part at the beginning (e.g., **BOOM! Your 50% off coupon inside**").

Next, use power words that tap into emotions like curiosity, urgency, and FOMO (e.g., "**Are you making THIS mistake with your Facebook ads?**").

And don't be afraid to get a little controversial or even downright weird sometimes (e.g., "**Why I'm giving away my $2,500 course for**

FREE today only"). Just make sure it aligns with your brand voice - you don't want to come off as a total psycho.

As for the body copy, it's all about keeping things engaging and easy to read. No one wants to slog through a giant wall of text, so break it up with short paragraphs, subheadings, and plenty of white space. And for the love of all that is holy, PLEASE use a conversational tone. Write like you're chatting with a buddy over beers, not like you're giving a lecture to a bunch of grad students.

One of the best ways to keep people hooked is through storytelling. And no, I don't mean boring-ass stories about your company's history or some crap like that. I'm talking about juicy, relatable stories that tie into your message and make your readers feel something.

For example, let's say you're selling a fitness program. Instead of just rattling off a bunch of benefits like "lose weight fast!" and "get shredded abs!", tell a story about one of your success stories. Paint a vivid picture of how they struggled with their weight for years, how it affected their self-esteem and relationships, and how your program finally helped them break through and transform their body and their life.

By the end of that email, your readers should be thinking, "Damn, if it worked for them, it can work for me too!" And that's when you hit 'em with the call-to-action to join your program.

But storytelling isn't just for promos - it's also a killer way to build a deeper connection with your list. Share stories about your own personal journey, your failures and triumphs, and the lessons you've learned along the way. Show them that you're a real person, not just some faceless guru trying to sell them stuff.

Of course, at the end of the day, you DO want to sell them stuff. That's where your promotional emails come in. But again, it's all about finesse. You can't just be like "HEY! BUY MY SHIT!" (I mean, you can, but it probably won't work out too well for ya).

Instead, focus on crafting irresistible offers that your subscribers can't help but say yes to. That means understanding their deepest desires and pain points, and positioning your product or service as the ultimate solution.

A few key things to keep in mind:
- Create a sense of urgency with limited-time bonuses or discounts
- Use social proof a bunch, like testimonials, case studies, and impressive stats
- Paint a vivid picture of what their life will look like **AFTER** they buy (e.g., **"Imagine waking up every day feeling energized, confident, and ready to take on the world"**)
- Make your call-to-action crystal clear and impossible to miss (e.g., **"Click here to get started for just $97"**)

And here's a pro tip: sometimes the best way to sell is by **NOT** selling. Huh? Lemme explain.

Every once in a while, send out an email that's purely value-driven, with no pitch at all. Maybe it's a killer blog post, a handy resource guide, or even just a funny story that brightens their day. The point is to show your subscribers that you genuinely give a damn about them, and you're not JUST in it for the money.

Not only does this build massive goodwill and trust, but it also boosts your overall email engagement. Because when people start to associate your name with valuable, entertaining content, they're way more likely to open and click on ALL your emails (even the salesy ones).

So there you have it, folks - the secret sauce to writing high-converting email campaigns that'll make your subscribers fall head over heels in love with you (and your offers). Craft a smart strategy, write subject lines that pop, keep the body copy engaging and story-driven, and mix in some hard-hitting promos with irresistible offers.

Do all that on the reg, and before you know it, you'll have an army of loyal buyers who can't wait to throw their money at you.

Chapter Six

Secrets of Writing Lucrative Video Sales Letters (VSLs)

W e're about to dive into the wild and wacky world of Video Sales Letters (VSLs). And let me tell you, when done right, these bad boys can be like a damn ATM machine for your business.

But why are VSLs so insanely effective at parting people from their hard-earned cash? It all comes down to psychology, my friend. You see, there's just something about video that taps into our primal brains and gets us all worked up and ready to buy.

Maybe it's the fact that video combines the power of visuals, sound, and motion to create a truly immersive experience. Or maybe it's because watching a video feels more like a face-to-face interaction, which builds trust and rapport. Whatever the reason, if you're not using VSLs in your marketing, you're leaving a whole lot of moolah on the table.

But let's be real - just slapping together any old video and calling it a day isn't gonna cut it. If you want your VSLs to convert like crazy, you need to put some serious thought into your script structure and storytelling.

First things first: you have to grab their attention right off the bat with a killer hook. This could be a bold statement, a surprising statistic, or even a juicy little story that leaves 'em wanting more. The key is to make it irresistible, so they can't help but keep watching.

For example, let's say you're selling a weight loss program. You might start your VSL with something like, "I used to be so overweight, I couldn't tie my shoes without getting out of breath. But then I discovered a weird little secret that helped me drop 50 pounds in just 60 days - without giving up my favorite foods or spending hours at the gym. And today, I'm going to share that secret with you."

Boom! Right away, you've got their attention and piqued their curiosity. They're thinking, "Damn, maybe that could work for me too!" And just like that, they're hooked.

Now that you've got 'em on the line, it's time to reel 'em in with some masterful storytelling. People love a good story, and when it comes to VSLs, the more personal and relatable, the better. So don't be afraid to get vulnerable and share your own struggles, failures, and triumphs.

Paint a vivid picture of what their life is like now, and contrast it with what it could be like after they buy your product or service. Use sensory language to make it feel real and tangible. And sprinkle in plenty of emotional triggers, like hope, fear, desire, and empathy.

For instance, going back to the weight loss example, you might say something like:

"I remember the day I hit rock bottom. I was getting ready for my best friend's wedding, and I couldn't even squeeze into my suit pants. I was so ashamed and embarrassed, I almost didn't go. As I stood there in front of the mirror, fighting back tears, I made a decision. I was going to do whatever it took to get my life back.

Fast forward to today, and I'm a completely different person. I have boundless energy, sky-high confidence, and a body I'm proud to show off at the beach. And the best part? I did it all without starving myself or spending hours on the treadmill. Imagine waking up every day feeling lean, strong, and unstoppable. Imagine being able to play with your kids without getting winded, or turning heads everywhere you go. That's the power of [insert your product name here]."

By the end of that story, they should be chomping at the bit to get their hands on your program.

But, of course, even the most riveting story won't do you much good if your offer falls flat. So how do you craft an irresistible pitch that practically forces them to smash that "Buy Now" button?

First, you have to load it up with value. I'm talking bonuses, discounts, exclusive perks - the works. Make them feel like they're getting an insane bargain that they'd be crazy to pass up.

Second, crank up the urgency and scarcity. Give 'em a reason to act **NOW**, whether it's a fast-action bonus, a limited-time price, or a cap on the number of spots available.

And third, back it all up with a rock-solid guarantee. Take on all the risk for them, so they feel like they have nothing to lose and everything to gain.

Here's an example of how you might put it all together:

"Normally, this program sells for $997. But because you took the time to watch this video today, I'm going to do something a little crazy. For the next 72 hours **ONLY**, you can get your hands on the entire system - the meal plans, the workout guides, the mindset coaching, all of it - for just one payment of $497. That's right, you're saving a whopping 50% off the regular price.

But that's not all. When you enroll today, you'll also get these three exclusive bonuses:
- Bonus #1: The "Rapid Results" Quick-Start Guide (Valued at $197)
- Bonus #2: The "Eating Out" Cheat Sheet (Valued at $97)

- Bonus #3: 30 days of FREE group coaching with me (Valued at $1,000)

That's an extra $1,294 in value, yours FREE when you join today. But act fast, because this offer expires in 72 hours - or when all 50 spots are filled, whichever comes first.

And hey, I get it. Maybe you're thinking, "This all sounds great, but what if it doesn't work for me?" Well, I'm so confident in this program that I'm willing to put my money where my mouth is. Try it out for a full 60 days, and if you're not absolutely thrilled with your results, just shoot me an email and I'll refund every penny - no questions asked, no hard feelings. You've got nothing to lose, and a lean, sexy body to gain.

So click the button below, fill out the secure order form, and let's get you started on your transformation today!"

See how that works? Value, urgency, scarcity, and a risk-free guarantee - it's like catnip for buyers.

So there you have it - the secret sauce to whipping up VSLs that sell like hot cakes and make you obscene amounts of money. Nail the hook, slay the storytelling, and make an offer they can't refuse.

Oh, and one last thing - don't be afraid to get a little weird with it. Some of the best VSLs out there are downright bizarre, with wacky characters, unexpected plot twists, and off-the-wall humor. As long as it grabs their attention and drives the point home, pretty much anything goes.

Chapter Seven

Mastering the Art of the Long-Form Sales Page

L et's talk about the mystical art of crafting long-form sales pages. Now, I know what you might be thinking - "Long-form? In this day and age of microscopic attention spans? Didn't we say long-form is done?"

But hear me out, because when it comes to selling high-ticket items or complex offers, sometimes you need more than just a snappy headline and a CTA button. You need to take your reader on a journey, my friend - a journey that starts with their deepest pain points and ends with your product as the ultimate solution.

But before we get into it, let's talk about when and how to use long-form copy for maximum impact. The truth is, not every offer is suited for the long-form treatment. If you're selling a simple, low-priced impulse buy, you're probably better off keeping it short and sweet.

But if you're selling something that requires a bit more consideration - like a premium course, a high-end coaching program, or a complex software suite - long-form copy can be your secret weapon. It gives you the space to fully articulate your value proposition, overcome objections, and paint a clear picture of the transformation your product can provide.

So, how do you structure a long-form sales page for maximum persuasive power? Well, there are a few key elements you'll want to include:

1. A headline that stops them in their tracks and speaks directly to their deepest desires or pain points. This is your one shot to grab their attention and make them want to keep reading, so make it count.

2. An opening story that hooks them emotionally and establishes rapport. This could be your own personal story of struggle and triumph, a case study of a successful customer, or even a hypothetical scenario that puts them in the shoes of someone who needs your product.

3. A clear, concise statement of the problem your product solves. What is the big, hairy, frustrating challenge your target audience is facing? Dig deep and get specific here.

4. A unique mechanism or "big idea" that sets your product apart as the ultimate solution. What's the one thing that makes your offer different and better than anything else out there? This is where you really need to nail your USP (Unique Selling Proposition).

5. A detailed breakdown of your offer, including all the benefits, and bonuses. Don't be afraid to get granular here - the more specific and tangible you can make it, the better.

6. Social proof out the wazoo, including testimonials, case studies, and any impressive stats or awards. People want to know that others have succeeded with your product before they take the leap themselves.

7. A risk-reversal in the form of a strong guarantee to take the pressure off the purchase decision. Stand behind your product and make it a no-brainer for them to say yes.

8. A clear, compelling call-to-action that tells them exactly what to do next and why they need to act now. Don't be coy here - if you want the sale, you gotta ask for it!

But simply having these elements isn't enough - you also need to structure your page in a way that guides your reader smoothly towards the sale. One of the biggest mistakes I see people making with long-form copy is just vomiting a wall of text onto the page with no regard for readability or flow.

Huge blocks of unbroken text are kryptonite for conversions - ain't nobody got time for that! Instead, you want to break your copy up into short, punchy paragraphs, use plenty of subheadings and bullet points, and sprinkle in visuals to keep things interesting.

Think of your page like a slippery slide - you want your reader to hop on at the top and whiz all the way down to the buy button without hitting any speed bumps or friction points. So make liberal use of "bucket brigades" (phrases like "But wait, there's more..." or "And that's not all...") to keep them moving down the page.

You also want to tap into the power of emotional triggers throughout your copy. Remember, people buy based on emotion first and justify with logic later. So don't be afraid to get a little raw and real with your language.

Paint a clear picture of the frustration, fear, or shame they're feeling right now - then contrast it with the joy, relief, and pride they'll feel once they have your product in their hands. Use sensory words to make it tangible and evocative. And don't be afraid to get a little "woo-woo" with it - the more you can tap into their deeper emotions, the more powerful your copy will be. Logic doesn't do that as well.

For example, let's say you're selling a premium course on how to start and scale a profitable online business. You might paint a picture like this:

"Imagine waking up every morning, rolling out of bed, and padding to your home office with a steaming cup of coffee in hand. You sit down at your laptop, fire it up, and check your email to find a flood of sales notifications from overnight. While you were sleeping, your automated funnels were working hard, siphoning money from the pockets of eager customers and depositing it directly into your bank account.

You smile to yourself as you think about all the lives you've touched - the single mom who was able to quit her soul-sucking 9-to-5 and be there for her kids, the college grad who paid off his crippling student loans in record time, the retiree couple who are finally able to travel the world in style. Knowing that your course made it all possible fills you with a deep sense of pride and purpose.

And the best part? You're just getting started. With your proven system and ever-growing passive income streams, the sky's the limit. No more trading time for money, no more begging for a raise from a boss who doesn't appreciate you, no more worrying about layoffs or recessions. You're in control of your financial destiny, and damn does it feel good.

So the only question is: are you ready to claim your slice of the online business pie? Are you ready to finally break free from the shackles of the 9-to-5 grind and live life on your own terms? Or are you going to keep settling for mediocrity, watching from the sidelines as others achieve the success and freedom you've always dreamed of?

If you're truly ready for a change, then I invite you to join me inside [Insert Your Course Name Here]. It's the exact same blueprint I used to go from broke and frustrated to generating over $500k per year in passive income. And I've distilled it all down into an easy-to-follow, step-by-step formula that anyone can use to achieve the same results.

Click the button below to get started, and let's build your online empire together. Your dream life is waiting for you on the other side."

See how that works? It's emotional, it's evocative, and it paints a crystal-clear picture of the transformation your product can provide. Pair that with a page that's structured for maximum flow and readability, and you've got a long-form sales page that practically prints money.

Now, I'm not saying it's easy - crafting high-converting long-form copy takes time, practice, and a hell of a lot of split-testing. But when you nail it, the payoff can be massive. And hey, if a knucklehead like me can do it, then you sure as hell can too.

Chapter Eight

How to Write Ads That Stop the Scroll on Social Media

This is where the big boys and girls play. Because if you can grab someone's attention in that half-second before they flick their thumb and keep on scrolling, you've got a shot at making some serious cash.

But here's the thing - writing ads for social media isn't like writing for any other medium. You're not just competing with other ads, you're competing with cat videos, memes, and pictures of your aunt's latest crocheting masterpiece. So if you want to stand out in the feed, you need to bring your A-game.

First and foremost, you need a headline that's gonna grab 'em by the eyeballs and not let go. And I'm not talking about some boring, generic headline like "10% Off All Products!" - I'm talking about a headline that's so intriguing, so bizarre, so damn irresistible that they can't help but stop and take notice.

One of my favorite formulas for writing thumb-stopping headlines is the "curiosity gap" formula. This is where you hint at something juicy or surprising in your headline, but don't give away the whole story. It's like you're dangling a little piece of meat in front of a hungry dog - they can't help but bite.

For example, instead of saying "Our New Skincare Line is Here!" (yawn), you might say something like **"The One Ingredient Your Dermatologist Doesn't Want You to Know About."** See how that works? It creates an itch that can only be scratched by clicking through to read more.

Another tried-and-true headline formula is the "how to" formula. People love a good how-to, especially if it promises to solve a problem they're facing or help them achieve a desired result. The key here is to get specific and focus on the benefit.

So instead of saying "How to Get More Leads" (boring!), you might say **"How to Generate 100+ Qualified Leads Per Day on Autopilot."** Now that's the kind of how-to that's gonna make 'em sit up and pay attention!

But of course, a great headline is just the beginning. You also need some seriously eye-catching visuals to go along with it. Because let's face it - people are visual creatures, and if your ad looks like a steaming pile of "meh," they're gonna keep on scrolling no matter how brilliant your headline is.

The key to creating thumb-stopping visuals is to make them bright, bold, and impossible to ignore. Think vibrant colors, striking graphics, and images that tell a story all on their own. And if you can work in some movement - whether it's a video, a GIF, or even just a little bit of animation - even better. Anything that makes your ad stand out from the static sea of text and images is gonna give you a major leg up.

But visuals alone aren't enough - you also need to make sure your ad copy is on point. And when it comes to social media, brevity is the name of the game. You've got a very limited amount of space to get your message across, so every word needs to punch above its weight.

One of the best ways to do this is to use proven copywriting formulas that are designed to pack a persuasive punch in just a few words. One of my favorites is the PAS formula - Problem, Agitate, Solution.

With this formula, you start by highlighting a problem your target audience is facing - something that really gets under their skin and keeps them up at night. Then you agitate that problem, really twist the knife and make them feel the pain of living with it. And finally, you swoop in with your product or service as the ultimate solution, the one thing that can take all their troubles away.

Here's an example of the PAS formula in action:

"Sick and tired of wasting hours every day on mind-numbing data entry? (Problem)

Imagine all the things you could be doing with that time - taking on higher-level projects, impressing your boss, even leaving work early to spend more time with your family. But instead, you're stuck in spreadsheet hell, watching your life tick away one cell at a time. (Agitate)

That's where [Your Product Name] comes in. Our revolutionary AI-powered data entry software can take care of all that tedious work for you, freeing up your time and mental energy for the things that really matter. With just a few clicks, you can automate your entire data entry workflow and start living the life you deserve. (Solution)"

See? In just a few short sentences, you've painted a vivid picture of the problem, made them really feel the pain of it, and then swooped in with your product as the ultimate savior. That's the power of a good copywriting formula!

Of course, there are plenty of other formulas out there that can work wonders for your social media ads. The AIDA formula (Attention, Interest, Desire, Action) is a classic for a reason - it takes your reader on a journey from initial awareness all the way through to taking action. And the BAB formula (Before, After, Bridge) is great for painting a picture of the transformation your product can provide.

But formulas alone aren't enough - you also need to make sure you're leveraging social proof and scarcity in your ads. Showing that other people - people just like your target audience - have bought and loved your product. This could be in the form of customer reviews, testimonials, or even just raw numbers (like "Join 10,000+ happy customers!").

You can create scarcity in your ads by using time-sensitive language ("Act now before it's too late!"), highlighting limited quantities ("Only 50 spots available!"), or even just hinting at high demand ("Our last batch sold out in 24 hours - don't miss your chance to grab yours!").

But even the most beautifully crafted ad won't do you any good if it's not reaching the right people. And that's where targeting comes in. Social media platforms like Facebook and Instagram give you insanely granular targeting options, so you can get your ad in front of the exact right people at the exact right time.

But with great power comes great responsibility - if you're not careful, you can easily blow through your ad budget without seeing any real results. So it's important to start small, test different targeting options, and really hone in on what works before scaling up.

And once you do find that sweet spot, don't be afraid to get a little creative with your targeting. Try targeting people who have engaged with your competitors, or people who have shown an interest in complementary products or services. You can even create lookalike audiences based on your best customers, so you're reaching people who are most likely to convert.

But targeting is just one piece of the puzzle - you also need to make sure you're constantly testing and optimizing your ads. This means trying out different headlines, visuals, and copy to see what resonates best with your audience. It means experimenting with different ad formats, like carousel ads or video ads, to see what stops the scroll most effectively. And it means keeping a close eye on your metrics - things like click-through rate, conversion rate, and return on ad spend - to see what's working and what's not.

The key is to always be learning, always be improving, and always be willing to try new things. Because the world of social media advertising is constantly changing - what worked yesterday might not work today, and what works today might not work tomorrow. But if you stay on top of the trends, keep testing and optimizing, and never stop learning, you'll be able to create ads that not only stop the scroll, but also drive real results for your business.

So there you have it - the secret sauce to writing ads that stop the scroll on social media. Craft thumb-stopping headlines and visuals, use proven copywriting formulas to pack a persuasive punch, leverage social proof and scarcity to create urgency, and always be testing and optimizing.

And most importantly, don't be afraid to have a little fun with it! The best social media ads are the ones that don't feel like ads at all - they're entertaining, they're engaging, and they make people want to click, comment, and share. So let your personality shine through, get creative, and don't be afraid to think outside the box.

Because at the end of the day, that's what social media is all about - connecting with people on a human level, building relationships, and creating a community around your brand. And if you can do that while also making some money? Well, that's just the cherry on top.

Happy advertising!

Becoming a Master Storyteller to Engage Today's Distracted Audiences

L et's get into the most powerful weapon in your persuasion arsenal: storytelling. And no, I'm not talking about the kind of stories your grandpa tells after one too many whiskeys - I'm talking about the kind of stories that grab your audience by the heartstrings and don't let go until they're reaching for their wallet.

You see, storytelling has been around since the dawn of time for a reason. It's hardwired into our DNA, a fundamental part of what makes us human. And when it comes to persuasion, there's nothing more powerful than a well-crafted story.

But why is that? What is it about stories that make them so damn effective at getting people to take action?

Well, for starters, stories create an emotional connection. They allow us to step into someone else's shoes, to feel what they feel and experience what they experience. And when we're emotionally invested in a story, we're much more likely to remember it, share it, and most importantly, act on it.

Stories also have the power to bypass our logical brain and speak directly to our subconscious. We might think we're making decisions based on facts and figures, but the truth is, we're mostly driven by emotion. And stories are the ultimate emotional delivery system.

But here's the thing - not all stories are created equal. Just like with any other form of persuasion, there are certain timeless principles that separate the "meh" stories from the ones that keep you up at night, wrestling with your credit card.

One of the most important principles is the hero's journey. This is the classic storytelling structure that's been used in everything from ancient myths to Hollywood blockbusters. It goes something like this:

1. The hero starts out in their ordinary world, going about their daily life.

2. They receive a call to adventure - something that shakes up their world and sets them on a new path.

3. They face challenges and obstacles along the way, testing their mettle and forcing them to grow.

4. They reach a climactic moment where they must confront their biggest fear or challenge.

5. They emerge victorious, transformed by the journey and ready to share their newfound wisdom with the world.

Now, you might be thinking - what the hell does this have to do with selling my product or service? But stick with me, because the hero's journey is a powerful framework for crafting persuasive stories in your copy.

Think about it - your customer is the hero of their own story. They start out in their ordinary world, facing a problem or challenge that's holding them back. That's where you come in - you're the one issuing the call to adventure, offering them a solution that will shake up their world and set them on a new path.

But just like in any good story, they're going to face obstacles along the way. They might have doubts, fears, or objections that hold them back from taking action. That's where your copy comes in - you need to address those obstacles head-on, showing them how your product or service can help them overcome them and emerge victorious.

And when they do take action and experience the transformation your product provides? That's the climactic moment, the point where they emerge as the hero of their own story, ready to share their newfound success with the world (and hopefully, sing your praises from the rooftops).

But the hero's journey is just one storytelling principle among many. Another key principle is the use of vivid, sensory details to create a rich, immersive experience for your reader.

Instead of just saying "our product will make your life better," paint a picture of what that better life looks like. Use sensory language to describe the sights, sounds, and feelings they'll experience when they use your product. Make it so real they can practically taste it.

For example, let's say you're selling a high-end espresso machine. Instead of just rattling off the features and specs, you might paint a picture like this:

"Imagine waking up to the rich, inviting aroma of freshly ground coffee beans. You pad into your kitchen, still in your cozy pajamas, and with the push of a button, you hear the satisfying whirr of the grinder, followed by the gentle hiss of steam. In just moments, you're holding a cup of the most luxurious, velvety smooth espresso you've ever tasted - the kind of coffee that makes you close your eyes and savor every sip.

No more rushed mornings spent in line at the overpriced coffee shop, no more settling for mediocre java from your ancient drip machine. With the [Your Brand] espresso maker, you can start every day with a moment of pure indulgence, a little slice of heaven right in your own kitchen."

By engaging the senses and painting a vivid picture, you're transporting your reader into the story and making them feel the benefits of your product on a visceral level.

Another storytelling principle that's especially powerful in copywriting is the use of social proof. Where you tap into the power of herd mentality by sharing stories of other people who have successfully used your product or service.

Think about it - when you're considering a purchase, what's more persuasive: a list of bullet points touting the features and benefits, or a real-life story of someone just like you who achieved amazing results?

Social proof stories work because they create a sense of "if they can do it, I can do it too." They make the benefits of your product feel real and attainable, rather than just abstract promises.

One way to use social proof stories in your copy is through case studies. These are in-depth stories that follow a customer's journey from struggle to success, showing exactly how your product or service helped them achieve their goals.

For example, let's say you're selling a weight loss program. A case study might go something like this:

"When Sarah first came to us, she was at the end of her rope. She'd tried every diet under the sun, but nothing seemed to stick. She was constantly tired, self-conscious, and fed up with feeling like a prisoner in her own body.

But then she found [Your Program], and everything changed. With the support of our expert coaches and the accountability of our tight-knit community, Sarah was able to break through the yo-yo dieting cycle and finally start seeing real, lasting results.

In just 6 months, she lost 50 pounds - but more importantly, she gained a newfound sense of confidence and energy. She no longer dreads shopping for clothes or feels embarrassed to eat out with friends. She's finally living the life she always dreamed of, and she knows she couldn't have done it without [Your Program]."

By sharing Sarah's story, you're not just making abstract claims about your program's effectiveness - you're showing real, tangible proof. And when other potential customers read that story, they can't help but think "if Sarah can do it, maybe I can too."

But case studies are just one way to use social proof stories in your copy. You can also weave in shorter success stories and testimonials throughout your copy, or even use user-generated content like social media posts and reviews to show the real-life impact of your product.

The key is to make these stories as specific and relatable as possible. Don't just say "our customers love us!" - share the nitty-gritty details of how your product has changed their lives. The more your readers can see themselves in these stories, the more powerful they become.

But perhaps the most important storytelling principle of all is authenticity. In a world of fake news and photoshopped perfection, people are craving realness and transparency like never before. And when it comes to your copy, that means being willing to get vulnerable and share your own stories - warts and all.

Think about it - who do you trust more: the polished, perfectly poised influencer who never seems to have a bad day, or the one who's willing to get real about their struggles and imperfections?

When you share your own stories in your copy - the challenges you've faced, the lessons you've learned, the mistakes you've made - you're not just building trust and credibility. You're also creating a deep sense of empathy and connection with your readers.

Because here's the thing - no matter how successful or put-together someone may seem, we all face struggles and challenges. We all have moments of doubt and uncertainty. And when you're willing to peel back the curtain and show your human side, you're giving your readers permission to do the same.

So don't be afraid to get real in your copy. Share the story of how you got started in your business, and the obstacles you had to over-come along the way. Talk about the mistakes you've made and the lessons you've learned. Show your readers that you're not just some untouchable expert - you're a real person, just like them, who's been through the fire and come out stronger on the other side.

And that's when the magic happens. That's when your readers start to see you not just as a brand or a business, but as a trusted friend and guide. That's when they start to feel like they know you, like you, and trust you - and that's when they're most likely to buy from you.

Chapter Ten

Productivity Hacks to Write More Copy in Less Time

Let's be real - as much as we all love the craft of writing, sometimes it can feel like trying to squeeze blood from a stone. But fear not, because I've got some productivity hacks that'll have you churning out copy faster than a squirrel on speed.

First things first - if you want to maximize your creative output, you need to develop a writing routine that works for **YOU**. And I'm not talking about some generic "wake up at 5am and write for 3 hours" bullshit. I'm talking about figuring out when and where you do your best work, and then ruthlessly protecting that time like it's the last slice of pizza.

For some people, that might mean waking up early and getting in a few solid hours of writing before the world starts clamoring for their attention. For others, it might mean burning the midnight oil and letting the words flow while the rest of the world sleeps. And for some unlucky bastards, it might mean squeezing in writing sessions between diaper changes and tantrum negotiations.

The point is, there's no one-size-fits-all solution. You've got to experiment and find what works for you. But once you do find that sweet spot, make it non-negotiable. Block it off on your calendar, set up a recurring appointment with yourself, and treat it like the most important meeting of your day.

But let's be real - even with the best intentions and the most iron-clad routine, sometimes the words just won't come. Writer's block is a bitch, and procrastination is her evil twin sister. But, luckily for you I have some ways to kick their asses to the curb.

One of my favorite techniques is the "word vomit" method. I'm talking about just letting the words flow without worrying about perfection or coherence.

Here's how it works: set a timer for 10-15 minutes, and just start writing. Don't worry about spelling, grammar, or even making sense. Just let the words come out in a stream of consciousness, no matter how ugly or nonsensical they may be. The goal is to get the creative juices flowing and break through that initial barrier of resistance.

Once the timer goes off, take a step back and look at what you've written. Chances are, there will be at least a few nuggets of gold in there that you can polish up and turn into something usable. And even if there's not, the act of getting words on the page will help get you unstuck and back in the flow.

Another technique that works wonders for beating procrastination is the Pomodoro method. This is where you break your writing sessions into 25-minute chunks, with a 5-minute break in between each one. The idea is that you're more likely to stay focused and avoid distractions when you know you only have to write for a short burst of time.

Plus, those 5-minute breaks are crucial for giving your brain a rest and avoiding burnout. Use them to stretch, grab a snack, or do a quick dance party to your favorite pump-up song. Just don't fall down the social media rabbit hole - that's a surefire way to kill your momentum.

But even with the best routines and techniques, sometimes you just need a little extra help to streamline your writing process. And that's where templates, swipe files, and other tools come in clutch.

One of the biggest time-sucks in writing is staring at a blank page, trying to come up with the perfect opening line or transitions between paragraphs. But the truth is, most of us are writing variations on the same themes over and over again. So why reinvent the wheel every time?

That's where templates come in. By creating a basic outline or structure for different types of copy - whether it's a sales page, an email sequence, or a blog post - you can save yourself a ton of time and mental energy. Just fill in the blanks with your specific details and voila - you've got a solid draft in a fraction of the time.

Swipe files are another game-changer. These are basically collections of high-performing copy that you can reference and draw inspiration from when you're feeling stuck. And the beauty is, you don't have to create them all from scratch - there are tons of resources out there where you can find swipe-worthy examples.

Just be sure to put your own spin on things and avoid straight-up plagiarism. The goal is to use these examples as a jumping-off point, not a copy-and-paste solution.

Another tool I swear by is voice dictation software. If you're someone who thinks faster than you can type (or if you just hate the physical act of typing), this can be a lifesaver. Just speak your thoughts out loud and let the software do the heavy lifting of transcribing them into written words.

Fair warning though - this can lead to some hilarious transcription errors if you have an accent or a tendency to mumble. But hey, sometimes those mistakes can lead to unexpected moments of brilliance. And if not, at least you'll get a good laugh out of it.

But perhaps the most important factor in writing productivity is your environment and mindset. If you're trying to write in a cluttered, chaotic space with constant interruptions and distractions, you're fighting an uphill battle. So take the time to create a writing space that feels good to you - whether that means a quiet home office, a cozy coffee shop, or a scenic outdoor spot.

And don't underestimate the power of a good mood. Writing is a creative pursuit, and creativity thrives on positive energy. So before you sit down to write, take a few minutes to get in the right headspace. Meditate, do some deep breathing, listen to a favorite song, or whatever else gets you feeling centered and inspired.

And if all else fails, remember this: done is better than perfect. Don't get so caught up in crafting the perfect turn of phrase that you never actually finish a draft. The beauty of writing is that you can always go back and edit later. But you can't edit a blank page.

Now, I know we've covered a ton of game-changing productivity hacks in this chapter - but what if I told you there was a way to crank your efficiency up to eleven and write high-converting copy in a fraction of the time? Well, I've got an exclusive bonus resource that's going to blow your mind and change the way you write copy forever.

Introducing **The AI-Powered Copywriting Playbook** - your ultimate guide to harnessing the power of artificial intelligence to create killer copy in record time. It's a cutting-edge, no-bullshit blueprint for using AI tools and techniques to write better, faster, and smarter.

Inside, you'll discover:

- Proven formulas for writing **high-converting** copy

- Plug-and-play templates to save you time and effort

- Insider secrets to make your offers irresistible

And so much more. Trust me - this is the resource you need to take your copywriting game to the next level and leave your competition in the dust.

So if you're ready to join the cutting edge of copywriting and start churning out high-converting copy in your sleep, then you need to get your hands on **The AI-Powered Copywriting Playbook** right now. Just click the **Learn More** button or **Scan the QR Code** below, and let's start writing the future of copy, together.

LEARN MORE
bitly

The Business of Freelance Copywriting: Getting Clients, Setting Rates, Delivering Results

L et's talk about the down and dirty details of turning your copywriting chops into a full-fledged, cash-generating enterprise. And let me tell you, it's not for the faint of heart or the easily discouraged. But if you're ready to roll up your sleeves, put in the work, and get strategic as hell, then keep reading, because I'm about to drop some knowledge that'll help you dominate the freelance copywriting game like a boss.

First things first - you need to figure out what makes you stand out in a sea of copywriters all vying for the same clients. What's your unique value proposition? What do you bring to the table that no one else does? Maybe you've got a background in a specific industry that lets you craft copy that speaks directly to that audience. Maybe you've got a talent for writing emails that get opened, read, and clicked like crazy. Or maybe you've got a personality that's bigger than life and infuses every piece of copy with your own special brand of wit and charm.

Whatever it is, you need to own it, hone it, and make it the corner-stone of your freelance brand. Because here's the thing - clients don't just want a generic copywriter. They want someone who understands their business, their audience, and their unique challenges. They want someone who can make their copy sing and their cash register ring.

But just having a unique selling proposition isn't enough. You need to make sure that every single touchpoint a potential client has with you reinforces that brand and positions you as the go-to expert in your niche. That means having a website that's not only visually stunning, but also packed with personality and proof of your skills. It means having a portfolio that showcases your best work and the impressive results you've achieved for past clients. And it means having a social media presence that's engaging, informative, and always on-brand.

So how do you go about crafting these key marketing assets? Let's start with your website. This is your digital storefront, your 24/7 sales pitch, and your chance to make a killer first impression. You want a design that's clean, modern, and easy to navigate, with plenty of white space and pops of personality. You want copy that's clear, compelling, and speaks directly to your target audience's pain points and desires. And you want to make it stupid easy for potential clients to see your work, learn about your process, and get in touch with you.

For your portfolio, focus on quality over quantity. Don't just throw up every piece of copy you've ever written and hope something sticks. Instead, curate a selection of your very best work, and make sure each piece is accompanied by a brief case study that outlines the client, the challenge, your approach, and the results achieved. Bonus points if you can include some glowing testimonials from happy clients singing your praises.

And when it comes to your social media presence, the key is consistency and value. You don't need to be everywhere, but you do need to show up regularly on the platforms where your ideal clients hang out. Share insights, tips, and behind-the-scenes peeks at your process. Engage with other professionals in your niche and build genuine relationships. And always, always, always keep your unique value proposition front and center.

But of course, having a killer website and portfolio is just the beginning. You also need a systematic approach to actually landing those high-paying clients and keeping them coming back for more. And that's where the strategies outlined in those resources come into play.

Let's start with networking, because while it may not be the sexiest strategy, it's still one of the most effective ways to get your foot in the door with potential clients. Attend industry events and conferences, both online and off. Volunteer your time and expertise to causes you care about. Offer to speak on podcasts or write guest posts for blogs in your niche. The more you put yourself out there and provide genuine value, the more opportunities will start coming your way.

Of course, if you're not a natural schmoozer or you're short on time, cold email outreach can also be incredibly effective - if you do it right. The key is to make it all about them, not you. Do your research, find a specific person to reach out to, and craft a compelling subject line and opening line that piques their curiosity and shows you understand their business. Offer a specific result or solution, and make it stupid easy for them to take the next step, whether that's hopping on a quick call or checking out a relevant case study.

But perhaps my favorite client acquisition strategy of all is building your own email list and newsletter. By consistently providing valuable, relevant content to your ideal clients and showcasing your expertise, you can build trust, credibility, and a loyal following of people who are primed and ready to work with you. Plus, you own the relationship and the communication channel, which means you're not at the mercy of algorithm changes or ad costs.

To make this work, you need to get crystal clear on who your ideal client is and what kind of content they crave. What are their biggest pain points and challenges? What kind of insights and advice would make their lives easier or their businesses more successful? Once you know that, it's just a matter of showing up consistently in their inbox with valuable content, engaging stories, and the occasional pitch for your services.

But of course, once you've got those clients in the door, you need to know how to price your services, negotiate like a pro, and deliver results that keep them coming back for more. And that's a whole other ball game.

When it comes to pricing, the key is to value your time and expertise, and not be afraid to charge what you're worth. That means doing your research on industry standards, but also taking into account your own unique skills and experience. It also means being transparent about your rates and your process upfront, and not being afraid to walk away from clients who aren't a good fit or who don't respect your value.

But pricing is just one piece of the puzzle. You also need to master the art of negotiation, and that means being prepared, being confident, and being willing to stand your ground. Do your homework before any negotiation conversation, and know exactly what you're bringing to the table and what you need to make the project worth your while. Practice your pitch and anticipate potential objections or pushback. And always, always, always be willing to walk away if the terms aren't right or the client isn't a good fit.

Finally, once you've landed the gig, it's all about overdelivering and building a long-term relationship with your client. That means being responsive, professional, and proactive throughout the project. It means going above and beyond to make sure the copy is not only technically sound, but also strategically aligned with their business goals. And it means following up after the project is done to make sure they're thrilled with the results and to plant the seed for future work.

Because here's the thing - freelance copywriting is not just about landing one-off projects and cashing the check. It's about building a sustainable, profitable business that allows you to do work you love, on your own terms, for clients who value your expertise and pay you what you're worth. And that takes time, effort, and a whole lot of strategic hustle.

But if you're willing to put in the work, stay focused on your goals, and always keep learning and growing, then there's no limit to what you can achieve as a freelance copywriter.

As the infamous Gary Halbert once said, "There is no security on this earth; there is only opportunity." So seize that opportunity, my fellow word warriors (was that one too corny? Sorry).

Chapter Twelve

Conclusion: Your Roadmap to Copywriting Success & Leaving the 9-to-5 Behind

We've covered a hell of a lot of ground in this book. From mastering the fundamentals of persuasive writing to crafting high-converting copy for every digital platform under the sun, from honing your productivity and creativity to building a thriving freelance business - it's been a wild ride, and I hope you've learned as much as I have along the way.

But here's the thing - all the knowledge and tactics in the world won't mean a damn thing if you don't actually put them into action. And that's what this final chapter is all about - distilling all those key lessons and takeaways into a clear, concrete plan that you can start implementing today to turn your copywriting dreams into a reality.

So grab a pen and paper (or fire up that Google Doc), because we're about to map out your personalized Roadmap to Copywriting Success - and kiss that soul-sucking 9-to-5 goodbye for good.

First things first - let's talk about mindset, because without the right mental framework and habits, all the tactical advice in the world won't get you very far. If you want to succeed as a copywriter (and in life, for that matter), you need to cultivate a growth mindset - one that embraces challenges, learns from failures, and always pushes yourself to be better than you were yesterday.

That means getting comfortable with being uncomfortable. It means putting yourself out there, even when it feels scary or awkward. It means being willing to take risks, try new things, and pivot when something isn't working. And it means surrounding yourself with people who inspire you, challenge you, and hold you accountable to your goals.

So take a hard look at your current mindset and habits - are they serving you, or holding you back? Are you making excuses, procrastinating, or settling for mediocrity? Or are you pushing yourself out of your comfort zone, taking massive action, and always striving to level up your skills and your business?

If you're not quite where you want to be, don't beat yourself up - we all have room for improvement. But do make a commitment to yourself, right here and now, to start cultivating those success habits and beliefs. Start each day with intention and purpose, whether that means meditating, journaling, or just setting clear goals for the day ahead. Surround yourself with positivity and inspiration, whether that means joining a mastermind group, attending industry events, or just curating your social media feeds to focus on people who uplift and motivate you.

And above all else - never, ever stop learning. The world of copy-writing and digital marketing is constantly evolving, and if you want to stay ahead of the curve (and the competition), you need to be a lifelong learner. Read books and blogs, take courses and workshops, seek out mentors and coaches who can help you level up your game. The moment you think you know it all is the moment you start falling behind - so stay curious, stay humble, and always be on the lookout for new ways to grow and improve.

But of course, mindset and habits are just one piece of the puzzle. You also need a clear, actionable plan for taking your copywriting skills and business to the next level. And that's where the rest of your Roadmap comes in.

So let's break it down, step by step:

1. Define your niche and your unique value proposition. What industries or markets do you want to specialize in? What unique skills, experiences, or perspectives do you bring to the table? How can you

position yourself as the go-to expert in your chosen niche? Take some time to really clarify your brand and your positioning, and make sure it shines through in all your marketing materials.

2. Build your online presence and portfolio. Create a website that showcases your personality, your expertise, and your best work. Share valuable content on your blog and social media channels that demonstrates your thought leadership and helps you attract your ideal clients. Curate a portfolio of your most impressive projects and results, and make it easy for potential clients to see the value you bring to the table.

3. Master the art of client acquisition and retention. Whether you prefer networking, cold outreach, or building your own audience through content marketing, develop a system for consistently generating leads and closing deals. Focus on providing value upfront, building genuine relationships, and always going above and beyond to deliver results that keep clients coming back for more.

4. Hone your copywriting craft and specialize in high-demand niches. Keep refining your persuasive writing skills, and stay up to date on the latest best practices and trends in digital marketing. Consider specializing in a few key areas where there's high demand and low competition, such as email marketing, sales funnels, or social media ads. The more you can position yourself as the expert in a specific niche or type of copy, the more you can command premium rates and attract higher-quality clients.

5. Optimize your workflows and productivity. Develop systems and processes for managing your time, your projects, and your client relationships. Use tools and templates to streamline your writing process

and minimize busywork. And always prioritize your mental and physical health - because burnout is real, and you can't pour from an empty
cup.

6. Scale your business and income. As you start to build a reputation and a steady stream of clients, look for ways to scale your
business and diversify your income streams. That might mean hiring
subcontractors or building a team to handle more volume, developing
your own info products or courses to generate passive income, or even
launching your own agency or consultancy. The sky's the limit - so
dream big and don't be afraid to take bold action towards your goals.

And throughout all of this - don't forget to seek out inspiration and
guidance from those who have paved the way before you. Study the
success stories of copywriters and marketers you admire, and look for
ways to reverse-engineer their strategies and tactics. Join communities
and networks of like-minded professionals, and don't be afraid to
reach out to potential mentors or collaborators. Because true success
is never achieved in a vacuum - it takes a village of support, encour-
agement, and shared knowledge.

So there you have it, my friend - your Roadmap to Copywriting
Success. It won't be easy, and it won't happen overnight - but if you
stay focused, stay consistent, and stay committed to your goals, I have
no doubt that you'll be able to build the copywriting business and
lifestyle of your dreams.

And as you go out there and make it happen, always remember the
wise words of my main man, David Ogilvy: "The best way to predict

the future is to create it." So go forth and create your own damn future, one word at a time. I'll be here cheering you on every step of the way.